A Study of the Gospel for Young People

MARK ROBERTS

Copyright © 2025 by Mark Roberts

2025: One Stone Press.
All rights reserved. No part of this book may be reproduced in any form without written permission of the publisher.

Front cover and inside layout by Noah Diestelkamp

Published by:
One Stone Press
979 Lovers Lane
Bowling Green, KY 42103

Printed in the United States of America

ISBN: 978-1-966992-04-2

1 (800) 428-0121
www.onestone.com

Contents

Introduction: Am I Ready?   1

Lesson 1: Can Young People Really be Christians?   3

Lesson 2: Why Do I Need to Become a Christian?   9

Lesson 3: God's Plan of Salvation   15

Lesson 4: What Does it Mean to be a Christian?   21

Lesson 5: Final Questions and Answers   27

AM I READY?

A study of the Gospel for Young People

> **PARENTS BEGIN HERE.**
>
> *THIS MATERIAL IS FOR PARENTS' EYES ONLY.*
> REMOVE BEFORE GIVING THIS BOOK TO YOUR CHILD.

It is the classic dilemma. For nine years Bill and Mary have been taking their son Joey to church services, reading the Bible to him at home and doing just about anything and everything possible to instill biblical values and faith in him. Apparently, it worked because Joey now wants to be baptized. Yet instead of being overjoyed Bill and Mary are terrified. "He's only nine — is that old enough?" Bill continues, "Do you really think he knows what he is doing?" Mary interrupts to ask "What if we discourage him now and then later he doesn't . . . . " She dares not finish that thought.

It is a tough place to be in. Questions swirl around us as we try to make the best decisions possible. We want our children to become Christians but only if they are really ready for that commitment. We don't want to say "No, you're not old enough" and end up turning a child against Christianity forever. What can be done? In some ways it is like working a jigsaw puzzle without the picture to look at. We aren't even sure we have all the pieces!

This book was written in response to this serious problem. There is a host of evangelism material on the market to teach the Gospel to adults (I even wrote some of it!). However, I know of not a single workbook designed to help young people understand the Gospel or assess their readiness to become a Christian. This book is designed specifically for young people who have grown up going to church all their lives, whose parents are Christians, and who are now thinking very seriously about becoming a Christian as well. If you and your child fit that description, then studying this workbook will give you a much better idea of your child's readiness to obey the Gospel.

Let me explain the plan of attack that we will use in this study. There are basically three essential areas that must be covered for a person to render proper obedience to the Gospel. First, one must know the facts of the Gospel message. This involves learning the biblical data about Jesus' death and resurrection, God's grace, and of course, our response to it. Second, there must be a personal appropriation of those truths. This is done primarily through the realization that I have sinned and I am a sinner who needs salvation. Third, there is the discussion of the life of the Christian and one's willingness to commit to that life and lifestyle.

Remove before giving to your child

i

Am I Ready?

This book tries to explore all three of these areas. You will find, however, the first area is not our primary area of concern. Most children "raised in the church" can recite the five steps of salvation backward and forward. They know what baptism is for and that one must be baptized to be saved. They have heard this all their lives and can recite (or regurgitate!) the data practically on command. *Yet, we still sense knowing the facts of the Gospel alone is not enough to qualify one to be a Christian.* Those feelings are correct. I know seven-year old children who can tell you the five steps to become a Christian, but they are far from ready to become a Christian! This is why this book emphasizes the second area: the personal appropriation of the truths of Christianity. This is, without question, the most difficult area to gauge and measure but is without doubt one of the most important components of becoming a true New Testament Christian. To be a fit candidate for baptism, one must not only know baptism washes away sins (area one), but that it will wash away *his or her* sins. A person must have a sense of brokenness and shame for sin (note Acts 2:37; 9:9). It is this awareness of personal sin and wrongdoing that causes people to want to be saved. Without it, baptism becomes a show that gains little. Ultimately, such a person's "Christianity" will be empty because he or she never knelt at the foot of the cross in the first place.

Throughout this book I have therefore tried to create "check points" where you, as the parent, can see if your child is truly aware that he or she is a sinner. These are marked with a star [★]. You will see as you examine those questions that we are looking for a sense of sinfulness, for an understanding of what sin is and the ability to say "I am a sinner." It is not enough to know "everybody sins" or "Jesus died for the whole world." Does your child know that he or she is a sinner? Do they understand that Jesus died for them personally? Are they personally convicted of sin? Do they term themselves as lost, and if so, why? This is what the marked questions look for and lead to. Watch carefully how your child responds to those questions. Obviously, no one can read the mind of another (1 Cor. 2:11), but these questions are the most important questions in the book. Many children know the facts of the Gospel and will agree to live the life of a Christian. It is this middle area ("Do they *get* it?") that is the toughest to gauge. These questions will help you get some measure of your child's thinking in this critical area.

Finally, the book discusses at length the life of a Christian (area 3). It is important no one come to Christ who does not fully understand the sacrifices and lifestyle required (Luke 14:26ff). Christians do certain things (like pay attention in the worship assembly instead of color or play with toys!) and if your child is not ready to do those things, then he or she is not ready to be a Christian.

Naturally, I cannot emphasize enough how important it is that you let your child answer these questions on their own. If you "feed" your child the "right" answers here, then you effectively short-circuit everything this book was designed to do. You might as well go dunk your child now — this book won't help you truly decide if your child is ready to be a

Remove before giving to your child

Christian. Nothing is gained by "rigging the game" to get the results mom and dad have already decided they want. You must be honest here and admit that studying this material with your child may indicate clearly that he or she isn't ready. Are you ready for that?

By the time you and your child have completed these lessons many of the pieces of the puzzle will be falling into place. The picture you see may be a child who is very mature, very aware of sin, and very ready to obey the Gospel. It will then be a delight to see such a child baptized into Christ. However, the picture you see after finishing up these studies (or simply losing interest in them after a few lessons) may well be the picture of a child who still isn't ready to make the kind of mature commitment to Christ that Christianity is. If so, put the book aside for a while, keep training your child and see if, in time, their heart will be better able to receive and understand all that the Gospel is.

May the Lord bless you as you raise your children to be His children. And may this little book contribute in some way to bringing young hearts to Jesus.

– Mark Roberts

Am I Ready?

Ideas for Using this Book

1. Set aside a regular time to study together. You may choose to study a lesson a day in five straight days. Better results may be achieved if some time is given between lessons for the material to "soak in." A child who can stick with this workbook for five weeks in a row is a child determined to become a Christian! A child who cannot complete the lessons over a period of time probably lacks the maturity and desire necessary to truly be a Christian. Watch your child to see how eager and enthusiastic he/she remains in doing these studies.

2. Let your child initiate as much of the study as possible. Do not badger the child to get the lessons done or complete them. If the youngster doesn't want to study and do the work necessary to learn the Gospel do not push him/her.

3. Some ask what to do if their child cannot fill in the blanks, run the references, etc? Is it not so that if a child cannot do the rudimentary things necessary as a Christian he/she is not ready yet to be a Christian? To repeat what was said above in a slightly different vein: a child who cannot do the workbook, or who will not do the workbook, is a child who is not *that* interested in being a Christian.

4. Once it is done, keep the workbook. Years and time will pass and your child will wonder if he/she did the right thing for the right reasons. A quick glance through these pages will assure your child's heart even if passing time has dimmed his or her memory.

5. Try to make the study enjoyable and free of a feeling of pressure. While this is very serious material your child likely will not benefit from a "final exam" kind of feeling as he/she works the lessons.

Remove before giving to your child

AM I READY?
A study of the Gospel for Young People

How old do you have to be to become a Christian? What does it feel like to be baptized? Do you have to "do it" in front of the whole church? If I became a Christian how would I have to change my life? Young people have a lot of questions about becoming a Christian, don't they? This study book will help you answer your questions about Christianity. You will learn what the Bible teaches about the Gospel of Jesus Christ and how to respond to it. You will also learn a lot about yourself, and whether you are ready to obey the Gospel and be a Christian. This is a serious study but you will enjoy working in the Bible and learning so much about such an important subject. Work closely with your parents (or the one teaching this study), and you will be able to complete these lessons and learn God's will for your life. Let's begin by seeing what you already know. Answer each of these questions as briefly, truthfully, and quickly as possible.

1. **T or F:** The Bible teaches you must be at least 12 years old to become a Christian. If you answered false, what is the youngest age a person can become a Christian? ____

2. What is faith?

3. If a person has some water sprinkled or poured over their head is that baptism?

★ 4. What does it mean to repent of sin?

5. Christians are, in many ways, different from people who don't care about Jesus. How will you be different if you become a Christian?

6. What does baptism do?

Am I Ready?

    7. Does a person have to understand the whole Bible before they can be a Christian?

★ 8. Have you ever sinned? If so, can you list any sins you have committed?

★ 9. Which of the following best describes you right now:
    A. A good person who does right most of the time.
    B. I don't do everything right but mostly I do good things and God is pleased with me.
    C. I have done wrong and the good things I do can't make up for them.
    D. A sinner.

  10. Why do you want to be baptized?

  11. Why did Jesus die on the cross?

  12. What does it mean for a person to "be lost"? Are you lost?

  13. Can you list the five steps of salvation?

★ 14. What is a sinner?

    Now, let's move into the lessons and start learning the Bible's answers to those questions! Study each lesson carefully, using your Bible as the lessons direct. Write any questions or extra thoughts you might have in the margins. May the Lord bless you as you study His Word and obey it.

LESSON 1

Am I Ready?

Can Young People Really be Christians?

INTRODUCTION

   A. *In the local church who does almost everything?*
      1. Adults do. They do all the teaching, participate in the worship services, and make all the decisions.
      2. This can lead a young person to wonder if Christianity is for adults only.
      3. Can young people be *real* Christians, actually serving and pleasing God?

   B. **Lesson objectives:**
      1. Learn it is possible to serve the Lord while young.
      2. Understand what it takes to be a servant of God at an early age.

I. BIBLE EXAMPLES OF YOUTH WHO SERVED THE LORD

   A. The Bible has many examples of young people who served God in ways that were very important.

   B. Joseph
      1. Read Genesis 37:2. How old was Joseph when we first meet him? _____
      2. Now read Genesis 37:12-28. What happened to Joseph?
      3. In this difficult situation it would have been easy for Joseph to decide that to survive he would have to worship Egyptian idols or to decide that since his parents were not there to watch him he could do whatever he wanted, even sin.
      4. Read Genesis 39:8-9. Did Joseph stop doing right just because he was in a difficult situation? _____
      5. Years passed, but Joseph finally had a chance to better himself. He was given the opportunity to interpret the dreams of the Pharaoh! Did Joseph forget God (see Gen. 41:16)? _____
      6. Joseph was a faithful servant to God even far from home — and God used him to save Egypt and his family from famine.

Am I Ready?

C. Timothy
1. Read 1 Timothy 4:12. Was Timothy old or young? _____
2. Nothing is ever said of Timothy's father. His mother and grandmother helped him learn what was right and encouraged him to do it.
3. What had Timothy learned even as a young boy that helped him be a faithful servant of the Lord (see 2 Tim. 3:14-15)? _____
4. Timothy became one of the apostle Paul's great helpers and carried on the work of preaching the Gospel after Paul was gone. He did all this even though he was a young person.

D. Mary
1. Read Luke 1:26-38.
2. We do not know how old Mary was when the angel appeared to her. We do know that in biblical times Jewish girls married very early. Luke 1:27 says she was "betrothed" or "engaged" to Joseph. This was usually done between the ages of 14-16.
3. The message of the angel meant great changes in Mary's life. Being the mother of Jesus Christ was a huge responsibility! Mary also must have thought about Joseph — how would he react to what was happening?
4. Read Luke 1:38 again. Did Mary make excuses, protest or try to get out of doing what God wanted her to do? _____ What was her attitude?
5. Mary was very young when she was selected by God for special service. She was a faithful servant to the Lord.

> *These examples help us see that young people really can serve God. Serving the Lord is not just for adults!*

E. Daniel
1. Read Daniel 1:1-4. Was Daniel old or young? _____ How did Daniel come to be in Babylon?
2. Do you think Daniel was afraid, since he was taken captive to a foreign land? _____ Do you think he missed his home and his family? _____
3. Like Joseph, Daniel could have decided things were just too tough to keep serving God. He could have

chosen to act like the pagan people around him and serve their false gods. Read Daniel 1:5-21. Did Daniel quit serving God?

    4. Read Daniel 1:8. What was Daniel's secret to faithfulness? *"But Daniel _____ in his heart"*. This means he made up his mind to do right!

    5. The book of Daniel records many more of Daniel's adventures. He was a faithful servant of God all his life — and he started while he was young!

F. The Bible makes it clear: young people can serve God!
    1. God has always wanted, and always will want, young people to dedicate themselves to His cause.
    2. Major decisions in life are made while we are young. This is a very important time in your life.
    3. Read Ecclesiastes 12:1 and fill in the blanks: *"Remember now your _____ in the days of your _____."*

II. WHAT DID THESE YOUNG PEOPLE HAVE IN COMMON?

A. As we think about the lives of Joseph, Timothy, Mary, Daniel and other young people found in the Bible we need to ask: What was it about them that caused them to be such fine servants of God?

B. Faith
    1. We will learn more about faith in lesson three.
    2. But, at this time it is vital for you to understand faith's importance. Read Hebrews 11:6. Can anyone please God without faith?
    3. Write out what you think faith is:

    4. Bible heroes like those we have studied genuinely believed in God and were determined to obey Him. You must do the same.

C. Willingness to obey God.
    1. Most people live for themselves, doing what they want when they want to.
    2. This is called self-centered living, because life is centered on selfish needs and desires.
    3. The Christian life is built on doing what God says.

Am I Ready?

4. Read John 14:15. If we really love God, what will we do?
5. You must decide if you will do what pleases you, makes you happy, or makes you feel good, or if you will do exactly what God says to do because you believe He is God and must obey Him.

D. Courage
1. It is not always easy to obey God. Many people in the Bible were hurt or even killed because they obeyed God instead of men. This is called *persecution.*
2. Read Daniel 3:14-15. Do you think Shadrach, Meshach and Abednego wanted to be burned to death in Nebuchadnezzar's fiery furnace? _____
3. Read Daniel 3:16-18. No matter how afraid they were or how much they wanted to avoid a terrible death, Shadrach, Meshach and Abednego wanted to obey God even more. Did they worship the idol or did they do right? _____
4. If you decide to become a Christian and serve God, what will you do if your friends make fun of you, ask you to do things that are wrong, or laugh at you because you do what is right?

5. It is important that you understand that Christianity is not always easy. Sometimes being a Christian is extremely hard. Are you ready to obey God no matter how difficult or unpleasant it is? _____

E. Integrity
1. Integrity is who we are and how we act when no one is looking.
2. Sometimes it can be easy to do what is right when everyone is watching but when we are alone we may find it much harder to keep doing right.
3. Joseph is a great example of integrity. His parents had no way of knowing what he was doing. They thought he was dead. Joseph was on his own. Did Joseph do right any way? _____
4. If you become a Christian you will need to serve God at all times and in every place *because you are serving the Lord in your heart.* Are you ready to do this?
_____

III. CAN YOU SERVE GOD AS A YOUNG PERSON?

A. Yes, you can! You can be like Daniel, Joseph, Mary and Timothy. What do you need to do?
 1. You need to learn why you need to be saved.
 2. You need to learn God's plan to save you.
 3. You need to learn what the life of a Christian is like, so you can decide if you are willing to do what Christians must do.

B. Are you ready to learn this important information so you can become a Christian? _____

C. Lesson two will help by showing why you need to be a Christian.

LESSON 2

Am I Ready?

Why Do I Need to Become a Christian?

INTRODUCTION:

A. *What is the greatest problem in the entire world? What is the greatest problem any person will ever face?*
   1. Different people would answer those questions differently.
   2. Some might say world hunger or the need for world peace.
   3. Others might talk about money problems or the fear of crime and violence.

B. The Bible emphasizes one central problem as the great dilemma for all people for all time: sin.

C. **Lesson objective:** to understand what sin is, who sins and how, and what it means to be responsible for sin.

I. WHAT IS SIN?

A. Sin is breaking God's law.
   1. "Whoever commits _____ also commits lawlessness, and sin is lawlessness" (1 John 3:4).
   2. Can you give an example of sin, of breaking God's law?
   3. There are many different kinds of sin.
      a. We can sin by doing what God has told us not to do (for example, telling a lie).
      b. We can also sin by failing to do what God has commanded us to do (for example, missing worship services on purpose).
   4. "Therefore, to him who _____ to do good and does not do it, to him it is sin" (James 4:17).

★ B. Have you ever sinned? If so, how have you sinned? Be as specific as possible:

   _____
   _____
   _____
   _____

Am I Ready?

C. Sin began in the Garden of Eden when Adam and Eve willfully broke God's command not to eat of the Tree of Knowledge (Gen. 3:1-15).
   1. Since then, every responsible human being has likewise intentionally chosen to do wrong.
   2. "For _____ have sinned and fall short of the glory of God" (Romans 3:23).
   3. We are not responsible for others' sins, nor are we held responsible for Adam and Eve's sin. We do not inherit the sins of anyone else.
   4. "Behold, all souls are Mine; The soul of the father as well as the soul of the son is Mine; The _____ who sins shall _____." (Ezekiel 18:4).
   5. Each person is accountable for their own conduct (2 Cor. 5:10). What does *accountable* mean to you?
   _____
   6. Accountable means to be responsible for what one does. Johnny's dad tells him to stop playing baseball in the house. Johnny does not stop. The ball gets away and breaks a lamp. Johnny is accountable or responsible. Why? Because he knew what "stop" meant and was capable of stopping. He *chose* to disobey and keep playing ball in the house.

II. BEING ACCOUNTABLE BEFORE GOD

A. The Bible does not define accountability in a single statement or verse. However, several passages of scripture help us understand this important idea.

B. **To be accountable a person must have the ability to reason and think.**
   1. "Set your _____ on things above, not on things on the earth" (Colossians 3:2).
   2. "'Come now, and let us _____ together,' says the Lord, 'Though your _____ are like scarlet, They shall be as white as snow; Though they are red like crimson, They shall be as wool'" (Isaiah 1:18).
   3. Over and over, the Bible urges people to think and to reason about their actions—what those actions mean and how God will judge those actions and thoughts.
   4. Understanding God's law is an important part of accountability.

5. Key question: Billy was born with a severe learning disability. Even though he is now 21 years old, unfortunately, he still acts and thinks like a three-year-old. Is Billy accountable before God? _____

C. **To be accountable a person must have the ability to know right from wrong.**
  1. As our ability to think and reason increases, our ability to understand right and wrong increases.
  2. "But solid food belongs to those who are of full age, that is, those who by _____ of use have their senses exercised to _____ both good and evil" (Hebrews 5:14).
  3. Normal children have some thinking skills but cannot always tell the difference between right and wrong.
  4. "'Moreover your little ones and your _____. . . who today have no _____ of good and _____, they shall go in there; to them I will give it, and they shall possess it" (Deuteronomy 1:39).
  5. Key question: a four year old boy is told, *"Do not steal."* He does not know what stealing is or why it is wrong. In the grocery store he wants some candy so he takes it and eats it. Is he accountable for the sin of stealing? _____

D. **To be accountable a person must be capable of understanding that sin is a violation of God's will.**
  1. "Against You, You only, have I _____, And done this evil in Your sight . . ." (Psalm 51:4).
  2. Many people think of sin as something "naughty" or something that hurts other people.
  3. Some young people think of sin only as violating their parents' rules. Read 1 John 3:4 again. Is this the definition of sin the Bible uses? _____
  4. Sin may involve other people, but the real problem with sin is that it is against God. Sin is doing what I want to do instead of what God wants me to do.
  ★ 5. Have you ever sinned like that? _____ Can you give a specific example?
  _____

> *Being accountable is about responsibility and knowing you are responsible.*

III. KNOWING YOU ARE ACCOUNTABLE

A. How can one know that he or she is accountable before God? An accountable person . . .

Am I Ready?

B. ***Is able to think about God's judgment of their actions.***
   1. Small children do not have a very good understanding of God or judgment day. They are mostly concerned about pleasing themselves or their parents.
   2. The accountable person understands that all people will stand in judgment before the Lord (2 Cor. 5:10). Thus, serving God is of primary importance because God will judge us.
   3. A person old enough to be accountable is capable of realizing this, even if he or she deliberately chooses to ignore the fact of the coming judgment.
   4. Accountable people can think about their conduct and what God will say about how they acted.

C. ***Has a conscience that hurts them when they do wrong.***
   1. Small children can do wrong without feeling bad about it at all. Why don't they have any sense of guilt? They don't feel guilt because they don't understand what they did, or that it was wrong to do it.
   2. Accountable people are different. They do feel a sense of guilt when they sin.
   3. This feeling is produced by the *conscience*. The conscience is a God-given gift that corrects us when we do wrong by making us feel miserable.
   4. "Now I rejoice, not that you were made _____ but that your sorrow led to _____. For you were made sorry in a godly manner, that you might suffer loss from us in nothing" (2 Corinthians 7:9).
   5. The conscience is not foolproof. If we ignore feelings of guilt long enough, they will go away (1 Timothy 4:2). Does this mean what we did is then okay? _____

   ★ 6. Have you ever done something wrong and then felt bad about it? What made you feel bad?
      a. I hurt others.
      b. I disobeyed my parents
      c. I hurt God by doing wrong.
      d. I knew I had done wrong.

D. ***Is old enough to investigate truth and see how it applies to his life.***
   1. All accountability focuses on the idea of knowing and obeying truth.

2. Thus, to be accountable, a person must have the ability to find truth, understand truth and obey the truth.
3. He or she must realize what the truth means *personally*, in his or her own life.
4. Would we expect a five-year-old to understand the significance of Jesus' death, burial and resurrection? _____
5. Even if that five-year-old can recite Bible stories about Jesus, he or she does not understand what it means in his or her life. The five-year-old is not able to grasp the meaning of Jesus' sacrifice on the cross.
6. The accountable person knows Jesus died on the cross. But, more than just this, the accountable person knows *why* Jesus died and what that means personally.

★ 7. Ask yourself: who did Jesus die for? _____

IV. CONCLUSION

A. What do you think about accountability? Do you believe you are accountable before God? ___ What makes you say "yes" or "no?" Talk it over with your parents or the one teaching this study.

B. Accountable people who have sinned are lost (Isaiah 59:1-2).
   1. God in His great love has put together a plan to rescue sinful people from their own sins.
   2. Would you like to learn more about this plan? ____
   3. That will be the focus of our study in lesson three.

Am I Ready?

LESSON 3

God's Plan of Salvation

INTRODUCTION:

A. God has a wonderful plan to save people in sin so they can live with Him in heaven forever.
   1. Many misunderstand this plan.
   2. Some even teach false or wrong plans to be saved.
   3. It is vitally important that we follow God's plan and not a plan that someone just made up.

B. **Lesson objective:** Understand God's plan of salvation. *Note: this is a long lesson and may need to be divided into two sessions.*

I. WHAT IS GOD SAVING US FROM?

★ A. What is it exactly that we need salvation from? From what is God saving us? _____

B. Many people do not take sin seriously.
   1. However, the Bible shows us that violating God's will is a serious matter.
   2. "For the wages of _____ is _____ but the gift of God is eternal life in _____ _____ our Lord" (Romans 6:23).
   3. What does it mean to die? Does a person physically die every time they sin? _____
   4. Romans 6 is talking about spiritual death which means to be separated from God.

II. HOW CAN WE FIND JESUS' PLAN OF SALVATION?

A. Today God communicates to us through the Bible.
   1. The Bible is "inspired" which means "breathed by God." This tells us it is from God Himself.
   2. "All _____ is given by inspiration of _____, and is profitable for doctrine, for reproof, for correction, for instruction in righteousness." (2 Timothy 3:16).
   3. The Bible is not man's thoughts or ideas. It is the word of God!
   4. When we read our Bible we can understand how to please God and what to do to obey Him (see Ephesians 3:4-5).

Am I Ready?

    B. It is very important that we respect and treat the Bible properly.
        1. We should study it carefully so we can use it correctly: *"Be diligent to present yourself _____ to God, a worker who does not need to be ashamed, rightly _____ the word of truth"* (2 Timothy 2:15).
        2. We must never add to it or take anything out of it: *"But even if we, or an angel from heaven, preach _____ other _____ to you than what we have preached to you, let him be _____"* (Galatians 1:8-9). What does "accursed" mean? _____
        3. We must obey it. To reject God's word is to reject Jesus! *"He who _____ Me, and does not receive My _____ has that which judges him; the word that I have _____ will judge him in the last day"* (John 12:48).

    C. Thus, the Bible is our guide to see what is right and wrong.
        1. We must follow the Bible, not what most people are doing (Matt. 7:13-14).
        2. As important as parents are, they are not our final guide. If your parents tell you to disobey God's word what should you do? _____
        3. Not even our own feelings are our guide. Feelings can be wrong, or misleading (see Proverbs 14:12).
        4. We must follow the Bible and the Bible alone!

    D. The Bible alone contains God's plan to save you from sin. Let's see what the Bible says about being saved.

III. GOD'S PART IN SALVATION: GRACE

    A. Grace just means a favor, receiving something you did not deserve.
        1. Salvation is a gift from God; it is something none of us deserve.
        2. *"For by _____ you have been saved through faith, and that not of yourselves; it is the _____ of God"* (Ephesians 2:8).
        3. By His grace God does what is necessary for us to be saved, particularly the sending of Jesus to die for our sins (John 3:16).

> *Propitiation is not a common word, but it is not hard to understand. It simply means "to turn away wrath or anger."* **It means that Jesus turned away God's anger at our sin by offering Himself as a substitute. Jesus takes the punishment due us.**

Am I Ready?

B. The center of the Gospel message is what Jesus did at the cross.
   1. Many people know that Jesus died a terrible death at Calvary, but they don't know *why* He had to die. Do you know why Jesus had to die? _____
   2. Read Romans 3:23-25:
      a. Verse 23 - everyone _____, so that means that everyone is lost, or spiritually dead. Are you part of the people described here? _____
      b. Verse 24 - we can be saved (justified) freely by God's _____.
      c. Verse 25 - because Jesus is our _____, or atoning sacrifice.

★ 3. Read Romans 5:9. What saves us? *"His _____"* Read Romans 6:23. Who should be separated from God (die) for your sins? ____ Who paid the penalty for those sins instead? ____

C. Jesus *redeems* us from sin.
   1. Redeem means to buy back, or to turn something in and receive something in exchange.
   2. You may have redeemed a coupon for a free drink at a restaurant. You turned the coupon in and received the drink in exchange.
   3. Read 1 Peter 1:18-19. Peter says sinners were "bought back" from sin ("aimless conduct") with something very precious.
   4. It was not money that was used to redeem them, it was "*the _____ _____ of Christ*" (v. 19).
   5. Christ exchanged His perfect life for our sin-filled life. By doing this He "bought us back" from sin. We are redeemed, or bought back.

D. Some people are confused about this.
   1. They do not understand why Jesus had to turn away God's wrath by offering His life. They do not understand why Jesus had to buy us back from sin.
   2. Many people wish God would just pretend we had not sinned or just agree to overlook our sin.
   3. They fail to realize that God cannot be fair and just if He pretends sin is not real or important.
   4. What would you think of a baseball umpire who called bad pitches "strikes" because he didn't want to hurt the pitcher's feelings? That would not be fair would it?
   5. In the same way, it would not be fair for God to pretend our sins do not matter.

Am I Ready?

      6. Yet God wants to be merciful to us. He does not want anyone to be lost (2 Peter 3:9). However, He must also be fair and just.
      7. These requirements are satisfied in Jesus. The penalty of sin is paid (justice) but it was paid by Jesus, not by us, so we can be saved (mercy).

  E. It is very important that you understand salvation is God's gift.
      1. Being a good person does not cause God to forget our sins or forgive them.
      2. Nothing we can do — *nothing* — will ever cause God to owe us heaven.
      3. It does not matter how much you go to church, how good you are, or how many "religious" activities you do. Sin cannot be "worked off" by doing good things.
      4. Sin has to be forgiven. The price for sin has to be paid by Jesus' blood.
      5. This is what grace is about: we cannot earn salvation with what we do, we have to depend (trust) on what Jesus has done at the cross.
      6. Actually, this is very good news. We do not have to earn salvation. Salvation is a gift God wants to give, not something you have to earn.
      7. Salvation is *accepted*, not earned. Do you understand the difference?
      8. If a wealthy friend said, "I'll cover everything—your tuition, books, room and board—100% of your college expenses," would you think you earned that gift just because you went to class and graduated? Of course not. It's still a gift. But the gift means nothing if you don't respond by going to college and doing the work. Do you see how that's like receiving God's gift of salvation? _____

IV. ACCEPTING GOD'S GREAT GIFT OF SALVATION

  A. How do we accept the great gift of salvation? The simple answer is we obey God in faith.

  B. In our first lesson we saw that faith is necessary to please God. What is faith?
      1. Faith is strong belief (based on evidence) in something we cannot see (Heb. 11:1).

Am I Ready?

2. We cannot see God but there is powerful evidence that He exists. The world we live in has so much beauty and design built into it. The world's beauty says there must be a God who designed it (see Romans 1:20).
3. Our belief that God is real and that He is God is the heart of our faith. This faith moves us to do all God commands us to do.
4. Faith in Christ means believing God sent His Son, Jesus, to this earth to die for our sins (John 20:30-31).
5. Trusting or believing in Christ is just another way of saying we believe Christ will save us from our sins.
6. Do you believe Jesus is God's Son? _____
7. Faith is trusting Jesus to save us. Do you trust Jesus? _____

C. Faith leads to repentance.
   1. God wants to save us from our sinful actions. Therefore we should turn away from that kind of living: *"Then Peter said to them, '_____ and let every one of you be _____ in the name of _____ Christ for the _____ of sins . . . ."* (Acts 2:38).
   2. Repentance is not living perfectly. Instead it is the fervent desire to no longer be involved in sin that causes us to turn away from the sinful deeds of the past and live as God wants us to.
★ 3. Can you list some sins in your life that you will need to repent of (turn away from) if you are going to be a Christian?

   _____
   _____
   _____

   4. Repentance is our determination to live as Jesus wants us to live.

D. Faith leads to confession.
   1. *"If you _____ with your mouth the Lord Jesus and believe in your heart that God has raised Him from the dead you will be _____"* (Romans 10:9).
   2. What does it mean "to confess?"
   _____
   3. Confession is our willingness to openly state our belief and faith in God and His Son, Jesus.

E. Faith leads to baptism.
   1. Baptism is an important and vital part of becoming a Christian.

Am I Ready?

   2. The Bible says it saves us: *". . . which now _____ us, baptism"* (1 Peter 3:21).
   3. Baptism is not an outward symbol that we are already saved. Read Acts 22:16. What does baptism do?
   4. For your baptism to be pleasing to God it must be done correctly. Some people think pouring or sprinkling a few drops of water on a person is baptism. Read Romans 6:3-4. Circle the method most like burying a person:
      a. Sprinkling
      b. Pouring water
      c. Completely immersing someone in water
   5. Baptism not only forgives sin, it also places one in Christ (Gal. 3:27). Can anyone be saved outside of Christ? _____
   6. All of salvation centers around Jesus. Baptism connects one to Jesus, putting a person in the Body of Christ!

F. Faith leads to a faithful life.
   1. Baptism is not the end of a Christian's responsibilities. It is important you understand this and not think that once you are baptized your "ticket" is permanently punched for heaven!
   2. *"Be _____ until _____, and I will give you the _____ of life"* (Revelation 2:10).
   3. The Christian's life is different from everyone else's. Christians obey God, worship, pray and study their Bibles.
   4. The Christian tries to be more like Jesus every day (1 Peter 2:21).

V. CONCLUSION

A. You have learned both God's part and your part in God's plan of salvation as explained in God's word, the Bible. Is there any way this plan could be wrong? _____

B. Now we want to learn more about how Christians live. Let's see what it means to be a Christian.

Am I Ready?

LESSON 4

What Does it Mean to be a Christian?

INTRODUCTION

A. It takes more to be a Christian than just an understanding of sin and accountability. A person must be willing to live as a Christian (Luke 9:62).

B. Some think the life of a Christian is summed up in just going to church on Sunday. This is wrong. Being a Christian is the way one lives all the time.

C. But what do Christians do? How will your life change if you become a Christian?

D. **Lesson objective:** learn what being a Christian every day means.

I. CHRISTIANS ACT LIKE JESUS

A. The first, most fundamental, and most important key to Christianity is understanding that being a Christian is the process of changing self to be more like Jesus.

B. The New Testament stresses this in several passages:
  1. *"A _____ is not above his teacher, nor a servant above his master. It is enough for a disciple that he be _____ his teacher, and a servant _____ his master"* (Matthew 10:24-25).
  2. Discipleship means becoming like our Master, Jesus: *". . . to be conformed to the _____ of His Son"* (Romans 8:29).
  3. *"Because _____ also suffered for us, leaving us an _____, that you should _____ His steps"* (1 Peter 2:21).
  4. This is what Christianity really is all about: changing self to be like Christ.

C. In every situation the disciple thinks about Jesus.
  1. How would Jesus act in this situation?
  2. What would Jesus do?
  3. What would Jesus say?

Am I Ready?

   D. It is important we practice this kind of thinking regarding sin.
      1. Jesus never sinned (Heb. 4:15).
      2. If we are to be like Jesus, we must keep ourselves away from sinful activities and thoughts.
      3. We will not want to even get close to anything that might cause us to sin because we want to be *holy* or pure.
      4. *"But as He who called you is _____ you also be _____ in all your conduct"* (1 Peter 1:15).
      5. Jesus was pure, and so, we must be pure as well.
   E. If you decide to become a Christian then you have committed yourself to becoming like Jesus. This is what Christianity is.

II. CHRISTIANS WORSHIP GOD

   A. "Going to church" is not the sum total of all Christianity, but worship is important.
      1. Jesus described true worship in John 4:24: *"God is Spirit, and those who _____ Him must worship in spirit and _____."*
      2. Worshiping in truth means doing exactly what God has specified in worship. We will not add to God's commands or take away from them.
      3. What does it mean to worship "in spirit?" This means to worship with our minds and hearts actively involved in what we are doing.
      4. The Christian does not want to just "go through the motions" of worship. He or she wants to participate in the worship by concentrating on the Lord and what the acts of worship mean.
   B. Do you know how to be involved in worship?
      1. During the singing, the Christian will think about the words of the songs and what they mean. He or she does not just sing the words without understanding and really meaning them (see Eph. 5:19).
      2. During prayers, the Christian listens carefully so the prayer being led becomes his or her own prayer.
      3. During giving, the Christian thanks God for the blessings in his or her life, and joyfully returns some of those blessings to the Lord (2 Cor. 9:7).

> *Being a Christian will change what you do during the worship services. It's time to put away childish things and serve the Lord!*

4. During the Lord's Supper, the Christian thinks deeply of Jesus' death on the cross and what it means, and examines his or her own life to see how he/she is living up to the demands of Christianity: *"But let a man_____ himself, and so let him eat of the bread and drink of the cup"* (1 Corinthians 11:28).
5. During preaching, a Christian pays attention, trying as best as he or she can to understand the message and see if it's true (Acts 17:11).

C. All of this is done to reach the goal of pleasing God.
1. This is what worship is about: pleasing or honoring God.
2. Is it pleasing to God when we do not pay attention in church, choosing instead to color, write notes, or sleep? _____
3. If a person is not old enough to worship, is he or she really old enough to bear the responsibilities of being a Christian? _____

III. CHRISTIANS OBEY THEIR PARENTS

A. The Bible is clear on this matter.
1. One of the chief obligations of children is to honor their parents by doing what their parents say to do.
2. *"Children, obey your _____ in the Lord, for this is right"* (Ephesians 6:1).
3. What does "obey" mean? _____

B. Before becoming a Christian, a child may have obeyed his/her parents out of fear of punishment or even because he/she loved their parents.
1. When a person becomes a Christian he/she now has an entirely new motivation to do what his/her parents say.
2. The Christian will obey them because the Master, Jesus Christ, has told Christians to do so!
3. Can you see how it is incompatible with Christianity for children to be rebelling, disobeying, or generally giving their parents lots of trouble?
4. Be honest with yourself: are you ready to obey your parents as a Christian must? _____

Am I Ready?

IV. CHRISTIANS LISTEN AND TALK TO GOD

A. It is important that Christians communicate with God.
   1. Communication means both talking and listening, both sending a message and receiving a message.
   2. God does not speak directly to anyone today. He has spoken to everyone finally through Jesus, His Son (Hebrews 1:1-2).
   3. This does not mean, though, that we cannot listen to God.

B. We listen to God by studying the Bible.
   1. The Bible teaches us what God wants us to do and believe.
   2. *"All Scripture is given by _____ of God, and is profitable for doctrine, for reproof, for _____ for instruction in righteousness, that the man of God may be _____ thoroughly equipped for every good work"* (2 Timothy 3:16-17).
   3. New Christians are just babies. They need to grow up strong and healthy in the Lord (1 Peter 2:2).
   4. This growth can only come as they read, study, and understand the Bible.
   5. Christians who refuse to read and study their Bible are Christians that have cut themselves off from hearing the will of God!

C. Christians talk to God by praying.
   1. Over and over, the Bible tells us the value of prayer.
   2. *"If any of you lacks wisdom, let him ____ of God, who gives to all liberally and without reproach, and it will be ____ to him"* (Jam 1:5).
   3. God hears the prayer of the Christian and will respond to it: *"the effective, fervent prayer of a _____ man avails much"* (James 5:16).
   4. When Christians sin (and they do), they do not have to be baptized again. Christians can pray and ask forgiveness for their sins (1 John 1:7-9).
   5. Christians can also ask God for help in every part of life. Christians are to be regularly involved in prayer (1 Thess. 5:17).

D. If you are to be a Christian, you must learn to read your Bible regularly and pray regularly.

Am I Ready?

V. CHRISTIANS CARE ABOUT OTHERS

A. The first principle of Christianity is to be like Jesus.
   1. If we read the Gospels, we quickly learn that Jesus was concerned about others.
   2. He was concerned when people hurt or were sick - Mark 1:41
   3. He was sorrowful when others sorrowed - John 11:35
   4. He was interested in helping people who were hurt, lonely, hungry or in trouble - Matt. 9:36; 14:14; 15:32.

B. As Christians we bear the same responsibilities.
   1. "Therefore, as we have opportunity, let us _____ good to all, especially to those who are of the _____ of faith" (Galatians 6:10).
   2. "Pure and undefiled _____ before God and the _____ is this: to visit orphans and _____ in their trouble, and to keep oneself unspotted from the world" (James 1:27).
   3. Christians are concerned about others. They do their best to help people in need as best they can.

C. Jesus was particularly concerned about people's spiritual needs.
   1. Read the story of the paralyzed man in Mark 2:1-12. What did Jesus do *before* He healed the man's paralysis? _____
   2. What does this show us that is even more important than physical healing and health? _____
   3. Christians reflect this concern by trying to teach others about the Gospel so they will be saved. This is called *evangelism*.
   4. Note how this is the job of every Christian, not just elders or preachers (see Acts 8:4).
   5. If you become a Christian you will want to do the best you can to teach others about Jesus Christ.

VI. CONCLUSION

A. Becoming a Christian is a big step. Living as a Christian is a big responsibility.

B. Jesus never wanted anyone to be deceived or fooled about the cost of being His disciple (see Luke 14:36-33).

Am I Ready?

C. Do you have the will and desire to do what Christians do?
   1. It is extremely important for you to understand this part of the commitment.
   2. Christianity is much more than "getting baptized."
   3. It is a way of living and doing and being. Are you ready to *be* a Christian?
      a. Yes
      b. No
      c. Not sure

D. Our last lesson will look at some final questions many young people have about becoming a Christian.

LESSON 5
Final Questions and Answers

Am I Ready?

INTRODUCTION

A. By now you are thinking seriously about becoming a Christian.
   1. You understand the facts of the Gospel and what each step in the plan of salvation means.
   2. You are also beginning to understand the meaning behind Jesus' death on Calvary and what it means to be a sinner needing to be saved.
   3. But there may still be some nagging questions in the back of your mind.

B. **Lesson objective:** answer any last questions about becoming a Christian.

I. DO I HAVE TO BE BAPTIZED IN FRONT OF EVERYONE?

A. This is a common question among both young and old.
   1. You should know the Bible specifies little about baptism, except it is in water and by immersion (note Acts 8:36; Romans 6:4).
   2. There are illustrations in the Bible of public baptisms (like Jesus', Luke 3:21) and private baptisms (Acts 16:33).
   3. Thus, there is no requirement for your baptism to be public.
   4. You may be baptized before a service, after a service, or at any time you wish. It does not matter how many people, or if any people, are present.

B. However, think about the nature of the Christian commitment.
   1. Being a Christian cannot be something one does secretly. We live for Jesus without shame or embarrassment about it.
   3. "Everyone who _____ Me before men, I will also confess him before My _____ who is in heaven. But whoever _____ Me before men, I will also deny him before My _____ who is in heaven" (Matt. 10:32-33).

Am I Ready?

4. Jesus is clear: if someone asks you whether you are a Christian or why you won't participate in something sinful, you must frankly and clearly state your commitment to Christ.
5. This is what living your confession means (Hebrews 4:14).
6. If you are wanting to be baptized privately because you are ashamed of being a Christian or are afraid some of your friends might find out and make fun of you, then it is time to seriously consider whether you are really ready to make the full commitment to Jesus that Christianity requires.

C. **True or False:** If I become a Christian, I am ready to tell anyone who asks I have obeyed the Gospel and stand with Jesus Christ.

II. IS IT RIGHT TO BE BAPTIZED BECAUSE YOU'RE AFRAID OF HELL?

A. Some people are just certain being baptized to miss hell is not a good reason to be baptized.
   1. The Bible teaches just the opposite.
   2. Hell and eternal judgment are mentioned repeatedly in the New Testament. Every time hell is talked about in the Bible, it is presented in the worst possible terms.
   3. *"The Son of Man will send forth His angels, and they will gather out of His kingdom all stumbling blocks, and those who commit _____ and will throw them into the furnace of _____; in that place there will be _____ and gnashing of teeth"* (Matthew 13:41-42).
   4. These vivid descriptions are given for a reason: to discourage anyone from going there!
   5. Jesus mentions hell more than anyone else in the New Testament. He clearly teaches it is a place to be avoided at all costs.

B. Hell is a real place and people who reject the Gospel will go there.
   1. *"Dealing out retribution to those who do not know God and to those who do not _____ the gospel of our Lord Jesus. These will pay the _____ of _____ destruction, away from the presence of the Lord . . . ."* (2 Thess. 1:8-9).
   2. All accountable persons who refuse Jesus will be sent to hell.

3. Some cannot imagine a loving God doing this to anyone. However, whether we can imagine or even understand it, the Bible teaches it will happen.
4. These passages urge us to obey Jesus Christ and be saved, so we won't be lost eternally in hell.
5. If you are terrified of being lost in hell then you are having exactly the reaction the Bible is seeking from you!

C. Being afraid of hell is not the only reason to become a Christian.
1. As you grow in Christ Jesus other important ideas will motivate you to remain a Christian. You will come to better understand:
    a. The wonder of heaven and the great joy there (Rev. 22:1ff).
    b. The incredible love Jesus showed by dying for you on the cross (John 3:16).
    c. How sin is deceptive and not nearly as grand as the devil wants you to think (John 8:44; Prov. 13:15).
2. All of these ideas (and others) will play a role in your developing Christianity.
3. The fear of hell is often one of the first motivators in being a Christian because it is so easy to understand and taught in so many places in the New Testament.
4. No one should be ashamed to say "I read what the Bible said about going to hell, and I don't want to go there! What must I do to be saved?"

III. WHY SHOULD I BE A CHRISTIAN NOW? CAN'T I WAIT?

A. Some young people fully understand the Gospel and its meaning in their life.
1. Sadly, they put off obeying Christ Jesus.
2. If a person is not ready to serve Jesus, he or she shouldn't "fake it" and pretend to do what they don't really have their heart in.
3. But every young person should understand the urgency of getting ready to serve Jesus and then becoming a Christian.

Am I Ready?

B. You should become a Christian before . . .
1. You die - no one lives forever (Heb. 9:27).
   a. It is easy for young people to think death is only for the old. This is simply not true.
   b. Read Luke 16:24. Will there be any second chance to do right after death? ____
2. You become caught in a life of sin.
   a. Some people become trapped in all that sin offers. Drugs, alcohol, evil friends — all work together to keep them from being interested in righteousness.
   b. These people quickly decided that parents, teachers, friends, or preachers who tell them to stop doing evil are "weird" or "not cool."
   c. Read 1 Timothy 4:2. What happens to people who ignore their conscience long enough? ____
3. You make decisions that could hinder your ability to ever become a Christian.
   a. You are on the edge of adulthood, with its many exciting opportunities and options. So many of your decisions in the next few years will determine the course of your entire life.
   b. If you are not a Christian how will that affect your choice of career, school or mate?
   c. Wrong choices in these areas can keep a person from ever becoming a Christian by exposing one to evil influences, negative peer pressure or direct temptation to sin.

> *What will happen to accountable persons who wait too long to obey the Gospel and die unprepared?*

C. Remember what we learned in lesson one. Many young people effectively served God while young. You can too!

IV. WHAT SHOULD NOT STOP ME FROM BECOMING A CHRISTIAN?

A. Worrying that someone will think you are too young.
1. Some people may never think you are old enough.
2. We cannot allow the opinion of others to keep us from doing what is right
3. The important point is what does God think and am I old enough to understand His will for my life and what it means?

B. Trying to become a perfect person.
1. If you were already perfect you would not need to be a Christian at all.

2. Christianity is only for those who have sinned and who understand they have sinned.
   3. As a Christian, you begin as a baby in Christ and then grow, learning to master sin and temptation as you grow up.
   4. If you wait until you are "good enough" you will wait forever.
   5. Don't be afraid to bring Christ your life with all its sins.

C. Fearing you don't know enough Bible.
   1. In the book of Acts people heard one Gospel sermon and were able to respond and become Christians immediately.
   2. One sermon showed them that they were sinners, that Jesus was the Savior, and how they needed to respond to Jesus' grace.
   3. Is the situation so different now?
      a. Do you know you are a sinner?
      b. Do you believe Jesus is the Savior?
      c. Do you know how to respond to Jesus' grace?
   4. People in New Testament times didn't wait until they knew everything about everything in the scriptures and you shouldn't either.
   5. The Bible is an incredible book that you will never learn everything about it. If you are waiting until you "know" the Bible, you will wait forever!

V. CONCLUSION

A. This concludes our study.
B. You should wait to become a Christian until:
   1. You've talked with your parents. They know you best and can help you assess your maturity, your attitude, and your knowledge.
   2. You understand what it means to be lost in sin.
   3. You are ready to commit to Jesus Christ. Becoming a Christian isn't the end of the journey, it is the beginning. Sometimes it can be hard. Don't start unless you are determined to finish.

C. Search your heart carefully, and pray fervently about these matters. If you do this, you will know when you are ready to be a Christian. May the Lord bless you as you seek His will for your life.